NED MANNING is a writer of plays, films, short stories and books. His latest work, *Playground Duty*, has recently been published by NewSouth Books. He has written many plays including short and full length plays. His most recent short plays have been included in 7ON's anthology of monologues for performance *No Nudity, Weapons or Naked Flames* (Federation Press). His children's play *Alice Dreaming* (Cambridge) is being used widely in schools both in Australia and abroad. He has written an adaptation for ABC Radio National of *Women of Troy* which will be aired in December as well as a schools version of the same play (Australian Script Centre). Ned has written two plays dealing with the Stolen Generation, *Luck of the Draw* and *Close to the Bone*. Other plays include *Us or Them*, *Milo*, *Last One Standing*, *Kenny's Coming Home* (Australian Script Centre). Plays for schools include *Kim*, *Not This Little Black Duck*, *Gods of War*, *The Flash Stockman* and *The Bridge is Down* (Australian Script Centre). He has written ten plays for Bell Shakespeare's Actors at Work program. Ned is a member of 7ON and is currently working on a new full length play for adults.

In memory of Leo Coe and Huw Davies

Close to the Bone

NED MANNING

CURRENCY PRESS
The performing arts publisher

CURRENCY PLAYS
General Editor: Katharine Brisbane

First published in 1994 by
Currency Press Pty Ltd,
PO Box 2287, Strawberry Hills, NSW, 2012, Australia
enquiries@currency.com.au
www.currency.com.au

NATIONAL LIBRARY OF AUSTRALIA CIP DATA
Manning, Ned, 1950–
Close to the bone.
ISBN 9780868193892.
1. Title.
A822.3

Cover design by Trevor Hood.
Cover photo shows Billy McPherson as Robbie and Pamela Young as Naomi in the Q Theatre production. Photo by Geoff Beatty.
Typeset by Erin Dewar for Currency Press.
Currency Press acknowledges the Traditional Owners of the Country on which we live and work. We pay our respects to all Aboriginal and Torres Strait Islander Elders, past and present.

Publication of this title was assisted by the Commonwealth Government through the Australia Council, its arts funding and advisory body.

Contents

From the Playwright

Ned Manning

Close to the Bone grew out of four years work with a group of students at the Eora Centre in Redfern. Inspired by Ernie Dingo, the students decided that for their end of year production they would produce a piece which reflected their lives and interests. Following each workshop I would write a scene reflecting the day's work. Karen Vaughan and some of the other students worked on the music and lyrics under the guidance of Scott Saunders.

The culmination of all this was a highly successful season at the Eora Centre, directed by Lydia Miller with assistance from Rhoda Roberts and David Kennedy, followed by a tour to the Adelaide Fringe Festival and then to a number of NSW country centres.

Close to the Bone's first professional production took place on 4 June 1993 at the Q Theatre, and following that production I re-worked the text with the assistance of the Associate Director at the Q, Michele Fawdon.

I would like to acknowledge the contribution of all those who provided inspiration and ideas for this text: The Eora Centre students and staff, Ernie Dingo, Lydia Miller and Jenny Lovell and later, Helmut Bakaitis and the Q Theatre and finally, Michele Fawdon.

However, this is a play which has roots in Australia's history and whose story is of people who have suffered beyond imagination. My role has simply been to tell that story.

Close to the Bone is dedicated to the memory of Leo Coe and Huw Davies, a Koorie and a gubba, who worked together at The Eora Centre to help this play come to life.

Sydney, June 1994

Discovering Our Own Culture

Mark (Peacock) Leon

I was asked to write an introduction to this book for the purpose of giving you, the reader, personal insight into what it is like to be an Aboriginal foster child. I share much in common with the people and the story of this text, as I too was taken from my Aboriginal family and fostered into a non-Aboriginal home. Much of the academic literature written previously on the fostering of Aboriginal children gives only the bare facts by way of explaining and justifying the government policy existing at the time. Many of us have read this type of information before and are aware of the basic facts. I feel that my purpose here then, is to ask that you, the reader, Aboriginal or non-aboriginal, please look deeper than these facts and figures. I am saying that in order to fully comprehend what myself and other Aboriginal people have had to endure due to the fostering of Aboriginal children, to understand what it was like to be taken away from our people and to live for many years not knowing our true identity, one needs to get in touch with all the emotions; the frustrations, the tragedy and the joy of our lives.

Many of us are only now coming to know our families and their traditions. Many, like myself, were not told until our later years that we came from Aboriginal families. It is very difficult to be Aboriginal and be part of Aboriginal life when one has been brought up in a foster home. In many cases it has led to emotional conflict within us. We feel the push and pull between the two different families and cultures, values and religions as we try to make sense of our world. On many occasions however, we cannot. We ask the question, what is it to be an Aboriginal person? Many of us do not know. Those of us who can, try to contact our Aboriginal families. When we do, we try to gain knowledge of the culture, so as to understand where we come from and who we *really* are. This desire to know our true identity is strengthened by the fact that, in the past, the stories we were told by the government and our foster parents were in many cases a collection of lies and deceptions.

It can only be through books such as this that Aboriginal and non-Aboriginal people will be given the chance to read first hand what it was like to be an Aboriginal foster child. Also to realise what it was like to grow up separated from our biological families, our people and land. We were young children when most of us were taken away, there was no choice offered on our own part or to our families as to where we would be fostered. Most of us never saw our families again until many years later. This causes much anger in myself and many other Aboriginal people. It is this anger and the emotions we feel, that will give the words in this book the power to bring to light the untold history of Australia. A history that needs to be known by all Australians.

The most important aspect of this book, however, is that it gives the people who were victims of the government's actions, the ability to relate and express their memories and emotions. It enables us to release some of the tension and anger that we feel towards such government policies. To give our account of these times will hopefully ease the tension inside us all. In so doing, we might be led in a direction where we might feel as one with our people and culture again, and to become a part of the life in which we were truly meant to live.

Mark (Peacock) Leon
Worimi and Thungutti Communities
Koorie Centre, Univeristy of Sydney, June 1994

Close to the Bone was developed and performed by the students at the Eora Centre in Redfern on 24 September, 1991 with the following cast:

ROBBIE/ASSISTANT DIRECTOR	Pauline McLeod
NAOMI/CAMERA OPERATOR	Pamela Young
BETTINA	Paula Maling
KARINA/SHARON	Kateena Clarke
ROSE	Karen Vaughan
ENID BOULDER/NURSE/ SOUND TECHNICIAN	Jo-Ann Close
HARRY BOULDER/ MISSION MANAGER	Brendan Read
TRICIA	Elizabeth Wymarra
CATHY/MISS BROWN	Pearl Davern
DIRECTOR	Sue Fowles

Directed by Lydia Miller, David Kennedy and Rhoda Roberts
Designed by Lydia Miller
Lighting by Mark Howett
Sound by Doug Peters
Musical Direction by Scott Saunders

All song lyrics written by Karen Vaughan except *Redfern Song* which was written by Pauline McLeod, Scott Saunders and Karen Vaughan and *The Waltz* to which additional words were added by Shane McNamara for the Q Theatre productions.

Close to the Bone was first performed at the Q Theatre, Penrith on 4 June 1993 with the following cast;

ROBBIE	Billy McPherson
NAOMI/	Pamela Young
ASSISTANT DIRECTOR	
ROSE	Brenda Webb
BETTINA	Victoria Kennedy
KARINA/MISS BROWN/	Bindi Blomstrand
CAMERA OPERATOR/	
SOUND TECHNICIAN	
ENID BOULDER/SHARON/	Anita Plateris
NURSE/MUM	
HARRY BOULDER/	Shane McNamara
MISSION MANAGER/	
FILM DIRECTOR/DAD	

Directed by Richard Walley
Designed by Joe Hurst
Choreographed by Matthew Doyle
Musical Direction by Shane McNamara
Lighting Design by Chris Day

CHARACTERS

NAOMI	
ROBBIE	NAOMI's brother, a drover
ROSE	NAOMI's third child
BETTINA	NAOMI's eldest daughter, aged seven
KARINA	NAOMI's second daughter, aged five
ENID BOULDER/	Station manager's wife
NURSE	Actress
HARRY BOULDER/	Station manager
MISSION MANAGER	
MUM	ROSE's foster mother
DAD	ROSE's foster father
MISS BROWN	Office bureaucrat
SHARON	Teenage Aboriginal girl
TRICIA	Teenage Aboriginal girl
CATHY	Teenage Aboriginal girl
FILM DIRECTOR	
ASSISTANT DIRECTOR	
CAMERA OPERATOR	
SOUND TECHNICIAN	

SETTING

The play takes place over a number of years as ROSE develops from a baby to a young woman. Act One begins on an Aboriginal Mission then moves on several years to Bin Bin station in outback Australia. Act Two takes place in Redfern and Epping, two vastly different suburbs of Sydney.

Although *Close to the Bone* was developed as a musical, it can be read and performed without music.

PHOTO ACKNOWLEDGEMENTS: *p.vi - pic 2*: Billy McPherson as Robbie and the cast from the Q Theatre production, June 1993. *Photographer: Geoff Beatty; p.viii - pic 3*: Victoria Kennedy as Bettina, Pamela Young as Naomi and Billy McPherson as Billy in the Q Theatre production, June 1993. *Photographer: Geoff Beatty*; *p.xv - pic 4*: Victoria Kennedy as Bettina, Bindi Blomstrand as Karina and Pamela Young as Naomi in the Q Theatre production, June 1993. *Photographer: Geoff Beatty*; *p.xvi - pic 5*: Billy McPherson as Billy and Brenda Webb as Rose in the Q Theatre production, June 1993. *Photographer: Geoff Beatty*; *p.12 - pic 6*: Pamela Young as Naomi in The Eora Centre production, September 1991. *Photographer: Rose Simpson*; *p.20 - pic 7*: (top) Paula Maling as Bettina, Pamela Young as Naomi, Kateena Clarke as Karina and Pauline McLeod as Robbie in The Eora Centre production, Septiember 1991. *Photographer: Rose Simpson*; (bottom) Anita Plateris as Enid and Shane McNamara as Harry in the Q Theatre production, June 1993. *Photographer: Geoff Beatty*; *p.36 - pic 8*: Brenda Webb as Rose in the Q Theatre production, June 1993. *Photographer: Geoff Beatty*; *p.43 - pic 9*: (top) Karen Vaughan as Rose and Pearl Davern as Miss Brown in The Eora Centre production, September 1991. *Photographer: Diann Payne*; (bottom) Victoria Kennedy as Bettina, Pamela Young as Naomi, Billy McPherson as Billy, Brenda Webb as Rose and Bindi Blomstrand as Karina in the Q Theatre production, June 1993. *Photographer: Geoff Beatty*.

ACT ONE

WE INTEND TO SURVIVE

ALL: [*singing*]
>   Rooster crows as the daylight shines through
>   He won't be crowing today mind you
>   He's found himself wound up in uncle's stew
>   With the government cuts what else can he do

chorus   So gather my children and have a good feed
>   We'll eat up the proof of this unlawful deed
>   We're much too resourceful to be pushed aside
>   Keep an eye on your stock 'cause we intend to survive

>   My cousin he works from morning to night
>   For a few extra rations it hardly seems right
>   But when it comes time to eat he calls his neighbours
>   around
>   Cooks up the rations with the beef that he's found

>   Repeat *chorus*

>   A card game round here can last sometimes all night
>   You see the payers emerge at the break of daylight
>   And the manager don't mind he was in for his cut
>   On the mission it's a way to make a few extra bucks

>   Repeat *chorus*

>   A black man helps stop his people from starving
>   Farmers watch them die while crops rot in their gardens
>   Handing out these vegies to stop people's hunger
>   I'm doing them a favour as there's less to plough under

>   Repeat *chorus*

A dormitory on the Cherbourg Mission. NAOMI *enters. She is pregnant and very tired, she carries a load of washing with her. She struggles to sit, putting the washing down beside her. She picks out an item of clothing and begins to fold it.*

NAOMI: Oh, I can't.

> *She wearily flings the item back into the basket.*

Bettina! Karina!

> *There is no response. She looks around for her children.*

Typical, bet they're down playing in the dirt.

> *She stands and looks outside.*

Bettina! Karina!

> *She signals them to come inside and wearily sits down again. She rests her hands on her pregnant stomach and then takes a few shillings out of her pocket.*

A few shillings!

A FEW LOUSY SHILLINGS

NAOMI: [*singing*]
> Woken one night, by a knock on the door
> Sent away your husband, don't expect him home said the law
> A handful of shillings is all that he left
> He said he needs to drink, he needs to forget
> And I dreamed of a man who would love me and keep harm
> away
> But a few lousy shillings is all my dream's worth today
>
> Two children growing and one on the way
> No extra rations and now no more pay
> Last night I dreamed of a man who would love me and keep
> harm away
> But a few lousy shillings is all my dream's worth today
>
> A black man who drinks, has committed a crime
> A white man who profits, don't even get fined
> And I still dream of that man who said he'd love me and keep
> harm away
> But a few lousy shillings is all my dream's worth today

NAOMI: What am I meant to do with that! Bettina! Karina! Get in here. I'll give youse a belting. Bettina! Karina!

She sighs. She slowly looks around the room.

What am I gonna do on this Mission?

She rests her head in her hands. Her contemplation is broken when the kids rush in, grubby from playing in the dirt.

BETTINA: What's for dinner Mum?

NAOMI: Look at you. What have you been up to?

KARINA: Nothing.

The children begin folding the washing.

NAOMI: What are you doing?

BETTINA: Helping Mum.

KARINA: Yeah Mum, look what we got for you.

She brings a bright red apple out of her pocket and shines it.

NAOMI: Where did that come from?

BETTINA: Oh, a man gave it to us.

KARINA: Yeah.

BETTINA: A man on a donkey.

KARINA: Yeah.

BETTINA: He was riding past the Mission.

KARINA: Yeah, he's gone now.

NAOMI: A man with a donkey.

BETTINA: True Mum.

NAOMI: Was he near the Mission Manager's garden at the time?

KARINA: Yeah.

BETTINA: No!

KARINA: Sort of.

BETTINA: He wasn't anywhere near it.

KARINA: Was so.

BETTINA: God you're stupid.

KARINA: I never broke the window.

NAOMI: What window?

KARINA: She threw the rock that broke the window that...

NAOMI: I beg your pardon?

BETTINA: I'm going to bed.

NAOMI: You're not going anywhere. You been into the boss man's garden haven't you?

KARINA: We was only playing chasies.

BETTINA: The boys were teasing us.

NAOMI: And.

BETTINA: And they started chucking stones at us.

NAOMI: And you broke a window.

BETTINA: Sort of.

NAOMI: Whose?

BETTINA: The ah...

NAOMI: The boss man's.

BETTINA: Yeah, sort of.

NAOMI: You broke the boss man's window! What am I going to do now? He'll kill me, he'll cut off our rations. You bloody kids, I could... go on, get to your rooms before I give you the thrashing you deserve.

The kids disappear, happy that they have escaped their mother's anger. NAOMI *fumes, then she looks at the apple, smiles and takes a large bite.*

Not a bad apple.

There is a knock at the door. NAOMI *freezes, then frantically hides the remains of the apple.*

Who is it?

MALE VOICE: Sergeant Rankin.

NAOMI: Who?

MALE VOICE: Sergeant Rankin, the Mission Manager sent me down to deal with you, hurry up and open the door.

Full of fear she does. Her brother, ROBBIE, *stands in the doorway, his appearance delights* NAOMI.

NAOMI: Robbie! You bloody ratbag.

ROBBIE: G'day Sis.

NAOMI: You nearly gave me a heart attack.

ROBBIE: Got ya eh?

NAOMI: What are you doing here? You look terrific, been on a good paddock eh?

BOBBIE: Can't complain.

NAOMI: Where you been? Seems like ages since we seen you. The kids'll be over the moon.

ROBBIE: Settle down. You'll wear yourself out going at that rate.

NAOMI: Oh, it's so good to see you.

They hug, then look at each other for a moment.

ROBBIE: So, what you been up to Sis?

NAOMI: Very little.

ROBBIE: That so?

NAOMI: Yeah.

He pats her pregnant stomach.

ROBBIE: Doesn't look like you been up to 'very little' to me!

NAOMI: Dunno how.

ROBBIE: If you don't know now, you're in big trouble sister.

NAOMI: Go to buggery.

ROBBIE: Where's Lester?

NAOMI: Took off.

BOBBIE: Oh.

NAOMI: Fair while ago now. Ahh, good riddance! He never was much use. Even when he was around he was either workin' or on the grog.

ROBBIE: That sounds like Lester.

NAOMI: Yeah, the good ones get sent away and the bad ones take off.

ROBBIE: Is that his?

NAOMI: Nuh.

ROBBIE: Oh…

NAOMI: Its been a rough couple of years Rob. Tell you one thing though, there won't be any more of these.

She pats her stomach.

ROBBIE: Yeah, well, how about a cuppa, man'll die of thirst.

NAOMI: Oh, sorry. Typical me, going on about me troubles.

ROBBIE: Well?

He indicates a cuppa.

NAOMI: I'll chuck the billy on. How do you have it again? That's right, black isn't it?

ROBBIE: Just like me women.

NAOMI: And three sugars?

ROBBIE: When I can get it.

The kids burst in. They hug him affectionately.

BETTINA: Uncle Robbie.

KARINA: Robbie! Robbie!

ROBBIE: Well have a go at you two.

NAOMI: Youse should be in bed.

BETTINA: Aw Mum.

NAOMI: Don't 'Aw Mum' me. You know the trouble I'll get into because of you two.

BETTINA: Won't do it again Mum promise.

KARINA: Yeah Mum, promise.

NAOMI: I bet.

ROBBIE: They been playing up have they?

KARINA: No Uncle Robbie, we haven't.

ROBBIE: What'ya reckon Sis? Do they deserve a present?

NAOMI: No, but they're gonna get one anyway.

ROBBIE: Here you go, I got something for you.

He takes out two roughly wrapped parcels. The kids unwrap them. One has a rock and the other a stick. They try to hide their disappointment.

Well?

BETTINA: Thanks Uncle Robbie, they're…

ROBBIE: They're special those, they come from a very special place.

Silence.

NAOMI: Well?

KARINA: Where they from Uncle Robbie?

He winks at NAOMI.

ROBBIE: Can't tell you that.

BETTINA: They're…

KARINA: Really…

NAOMI: Interesting?

BETTINA: Yes, interesting…

NAOMI: Well?

BETTINA: Oh, thanks Uncle Robbie.

ROBBIE: And I got these, they're from a special place too.

He gives them a bag of lollies. The kids erupt.

KARINA: Whacko, lollies!

NAOMI *is delighted by all this. Her family are with her.*

NAOMI: You're bloody lucky you kids.
ROBBIE: They're all right.
NAOMI: They're spoilt.
ROBBIE: Why not? They're family. Here, give your old Uncle a hug.

They do.

KARINA: Thanks Uncle Robbie.
BETTINA: We missed you.
NAOMI: See?

ROBBIE *laughs.*

So, ratbag, where have you been?

WALKABOUT

ROBBIE: [*singing*]
Walkabout on the Brisbane Track
Trying to stay out of jail, keep the sun on my back
When things go wrong you have to fight
Do your best to make things right
Instead of paying me they just mocked
So I sold off some of their stock.

And went walkabout on the Lismore Track
Trying to stay out of jail, keep the sun on my back
When things get tough you still have to try
The harder it gets the more you learn to survive
And I got into some strife
Got caught with the Boss man's wife.

And I walkabout on the Moree track
Trying to stay out of jail, keep then sun on my back
When rules are made you know they're gonna be broke
White man's laws are just a bad joke
Couldn't use the toilet in the bar
So I went in his car.

Then went walkabout on the Macksville track
Trying to stay out of jail, keep the sun on my back
You do the same work you should get the same pay
But sometimes you have to find your own way
And I like to take what I'm owed
And they go and say that I stole.

Walkabout on those country tracks,
Free.

NAOMI: Now, time you went to bed. Go on! Get goin' before I give you something to think about.

They hug ROBBIE *and run off to bed.*

ROBBIE: Be good if we could stay that age don't you think?

NAOMI: I'll say…

ROBBIE: It was all so simple eh?

NAOMI: Yeah. Remember when we were kids?

ROBBIE: Just…

NAOMI: I'll never forget you riding that cow, or trying to.

ROBBIE: You used to look like a bloody monkey.

NAOMI: Thanks.

ROBBIE: True. You did, always climbing up trees and carrying on.

NAOMI: Used to be fun swingin' off that rope into the creek eh?

ROBBIE: Yeah. They were the days…

Pause.

NAOMI: When you going to get yourself a woman?

ROBBIE: Already got one for each day of the week, anymore'd knock a fella around too much.

NAOMI: Get out, I mean a good woman.

ROBBIE: They're all good women.

NAOMI: You ought to wake up to yourself. You need someone to settle down with.

ROBBIE: I got too much travelling around to do.

NAOMI: Oh yeah! You just like playing the field.

ROBBIE: Dunno, maybe I can't settle down.

NAOMI *looks at her brother and laughs.*

NAOMI: It's so good to see you bro.

She gives him another big hug.

Us mob stick together right?

ROBBIE: Right.

The MISSION MANAGER *walks in. He is aggressive and arrogant. At first he doesn't see* ROBBIE.

MISSION MANAGER: How's me favourite girl? Got a kiss for your old mate.

He grabs NAOMI *lasciviously and then sees* ROBBIE.

Who's this? One of your boyfriends eh?

NAOMI: This is my brother.

MISSION MANAGER: Oh yeah.

During the following, ROBBIE *adopts a subservient pose.*

ROBBIE: True boss.

NAOMI: He's just travelling through.

MISSION MANAGER: You haven't got a permit.

ROBBIE: Sorry boss?

MISSION MANAGER: Did you sign on?

ROBBIE: Sign boss?

MISSION MANAGER: At the office. You're not allowed on the Mission without signing on.

NAOMI: He's only…

MISSION MANAGER: You know the rules.

ROBBIE: Sorry boss, I can't write.

MISSION MANAGER: Don't get smart with me.

ROBBIE: Yes boss.

MISSION MANAGER: Where are those bloody kids of yours.

NAOMI: In bed.

MANAGER: They been playing down near my place again.

NAOMI: No, they've been here all afternoon.

MISSION MANAGER: Bullshit.

NAOMI: They have. Honest.

MISSION MANAGER : I don't believe you. One of my windows got smashed.

NAOMI: Wasn't my kids.

MISSION MANAGER: Yeah? Well, I'm gonna take the cost of it out of you rations.

NAOMI: You can't do that, we hardly got enough as it is.

MISSON MANAGER: Catch yourself a few rabbits, plenty of them about.

ROBBIE: How much was it boss?

MISSION MANAGER: What?

ROBBIE: How much was the window.

MISSION MANAGER: What's it got to do with you?

> ROBBIE *gives some money to the* MISSION MANAGER.

ROBBIE: Reckon this should cover it, eh boss?

MISSION MANAGER: Where'd you get this from?

ROBBIE: Workin' boss.

MISSION MANAGER: I don't believe you.

ROBBIE: True boss, honest.

MISSION MANAGER: I reckon you might have a bit of explaining to do.

ROBBIE: Sorry boss?

MISSION MANAGER: I'm going to let the police know about you. And make sure you're off this Mission by six O'Clock.

ROBBIE: I'm on me way now boss. Don't mean to cause any trouble boss. True.

MISSION MANAGER: You just watch yourself. I don't like the look of you.

ROBBIE: Sorry boss.

MISSION MANAGER: I'll be back to see you later Naomi. You keep a bloody good eye on those brats of yours, they'll cause you more harm than good. I don't know why you don't get rid of them. Your old man's no bloody good to you.

NAOMI: How'd...

> ROBBIE *interrupts.*

ROBBIE: You're right there boss.

MISSION MANAGER: Who asked you? You bloody well clear out of here before you get into strife. Christ, meant to be your sister is she? Why don't you look after her then?

ROBBIE: Don't know boss.

> *The* MISSION MANAGER *checks his fob watch.*

ACT ONE

11

MISSION MANAGER: You better be out of here before I get back from my rounds.

He goes to leave.

I never forget a face so don't think you're getting away with anything.

He leaves.

ROBBIE: Yes boss, no boss, three bags full boss.

NAOMI: Shhh. He might hear you.

ROBBIE: Okay. Okay. I better be going. I don't want to cause you any trouble.

NAOMI: Stay a bit longer, please. I haven't seen you for so long.

ROBBIE: No Sis, I don't want any gubba trouble.

NAOMI: He won't be back for a while...

ROBBIE: He'll be back all right.

NAOMI: Robbie, you gotta help me.

ROBBIE: How?

NAOMI: That fella, that Mission Manager. He keeps threatening me.

ROBBIE: He's a gubba isn't he?

NAOMI: It's more than that. He's been sniffing around here for a while. He keeps threatening that he's gonna come back for me after baby's born. I'm scared Robbie. There's been trouble since Les took off. Ever since then there's been no-one around to keep an eye out for me. You know what these blokes are like. God Robbie, what am I gonna do?

ROBBIE: I dunno Sis but I know what I've got to do and that's to clear off out of here as quickly as possible.

He prepares to go.

Don't worry Sis, she'll be right. Things always work out for the best. You'll see bub, you'll see. Don't get yourself all worked up. Maybe I can figure something out. I know what'll happen if I stay, he'll sool the gungies onto me and that's the last thing I need. You look after yourself and those kids. Hey, if the little one turns out to be a boy, I reckon Robbie's not a bad name!

With that he leaves. NAOMI *lets out a cry of anguish. She looks up as if adressing God.*

NAOMI: What are you doing to me God? What's going on? What have I done wrong? I know you've got a lot of people to care for God, but sometimes… I wonder, what's goin' on? I wonder if you're listening. Have you gone walkabout God? I mean, I know you're really busy, I know you've probably got a lot on your plate and you can't be everywhere at the same time but I wish you'd just spend a few minutes on me. Please.

SCENE TWO

Later that night. NAOMI *and the kids are asleep. The window is forced open. A figure climbs through. We cannot see the face but can make out that it is a man.* NAOMI *stirs.*

NAOMI: What's…

> *The figure covers her mouth. They struggle. The children stir. The figure reveals himself, it is* ROBBIE.

ROBBIE: Shhh. Don't make a sound.

NAOMI: What are you doing?

ROBBIE: I've got a mate standing by outside. We're gettin' you out of here Sis.

NAOMI: Where're we going?

ROBBIE: Just be quiet, we gotta get those kids out of here without making a sound. Don't want those bloody mongrels yappin' and wakin' that bastard up.

NAOMI: But…

ROBBIE: For once in your life shut up and do as you're told.

> ROBBIE *and* NAOMI *collect the kids and escape.*

SCENE THREE

ROBBIE *and* NAOMI *sit by a fire. They are watching the children playing on the river.* ROBBIE *threads gum nuts through some twine. He is making wrist bands. There are many sounds, bush sounds. Nightfall is approaching.*

ROBBIE: Hey, you kids, don't eat too many of them berries, they'll make you sick.

BETTINA: [*off*] These ones?

> *The kids laugh.*

ROBBIE: Don't come running to me if you get a gut ache. [*Poking at the fire*] Time for a brew eh?

NAOMI: Yeah, I reckon.

ROBBIE: Hey kids, bring us some water will ya?

NAOMI: Don't fall in.

ROBBIE: They'll be right, it's real shallow here, there's a sand bank runs halfway across the river. You only got to keep an eye on it after rain, then the current gets a bit strong.

NAOMI: Bettina's alright in the water but I worry about Karina, she never watches what she's doing.

ROBBIE: Relax Sis, you're not on the Mission now.

> *The kids run in with some water; they are obviously enjoying their newfound freedom.*

KARINA: Here Uncle Robbie.

ROBBIE: Thanks bub. Here, I got something for you girls. Something to remind you of the day you left the Mission.

> *He gives the girls a precious stone each.*

[*Patting* NAOMI'*s pregnant stomach*] And here's one for little Robbie in there.

BETTINA: I'm gonna have a swing off that rope.

KARINA: Me too.

BETTINA: What's for dinner Mum?

NAOMI: You wait and see.

ROBBIE: We might have a bit of snake eh?

BETTINA: Snake?

KARINA: Yuck.

ROBBIE: Or some berries, or some roo. You like roo?

BETTINA: I dunno.

KARINA: I do.

BETTINA: How would you know?

KARINA: I do.

ROBBIE: Yeah? Well, I got one buried in the sand over there.

KARINA: What for?

ROBBIE: What do you mean what for? To keep it cool of course.

KARINA: Why don't you put it in the fridge?

BETTINA: What fridge?

ROBBIE: The sand's a kind of fridge. If you bury things in it they stay cool. You kids gotta learn about the bush.

KARINA: Can we go and play?

NAOMI: Go on and be careful!

ROBBIE: You can play wherever you like, you're not on the Mission now.

The kids run off.

BETTINA: Bags the rope first.

ROBBIE: Watch yourself. Hey, Sis, talking about watches…

He pulls out the MISSION MANAGER'S *fob watch.*

NAOMI: Robbie!

There is a loud scream. The kids come rushing back.

BETTINA: Snake! I nearly stood on a snake!

KARINA: Mummy!

ROBBIE: Hey, you take it easy. Don't scare the snake. He might run off. Where'd you see him?

KARINA: Over there.

ROBBIE: He probably gone now, all that noise. Don't move.

ROBBIE *steathily hunts the snake. He catches it.*

Tucker! He's a big fat lazy fella. Not many snakes hang around after all that, they don't like noise and carryin' on. You make a bit of noise when you're walking along and he'll piss off, he's more scared of you than you are of him.

The kids are frozen.

Go on, off you go. The river's nice and shallow, been no rain. Best time to play.

KARINA: Maybe after.

ROBBIE: Go on, I'll give you a yell when the tucker's ready.

The kids leave, this time with extreme caution. The sight of them tip-toeing makes ROBBIE *laugh.*

They're a couple of good 'uns those two.

NAOMI: It's so good to be free, eh Rob?

ROBBIE: Mission's no place for you Sis.

He stokes the fire, boiling the water.

Cup of real tea eh? Billy tea.

NAOMI: Where'd the tea come from?

ROBBIE *smiles. He busies himself making the tea.*

ROBBIE: I better see if this roo is okay while I'm at it eh? What do you reckon? Good cup a billy tea, bit of fried snake and some roo meat, sounds like pretty good tucker to me. Here, you can skin this.

He chucks the snake to Naomi.

Still remember how?

NAOMI: What do you reckon?

She skins the snake expertly as ROBBIE *digs up the roo.*

Where we going Robbie?

ROBBIE: Place called Bin Bin Station. I done a lot of droving work there. They're a good mob. 'Specially the Mrs Old Harry's a bit of a mongrel but no-one takes too much notice of him. A lot of blackfellas work on the place, the pay's good and the tucker's not too bad. We do all the stock work for old Harry. He doesn't know too much about it so he usually leaves it up to me. His manager's a good bloke, reckon he's got a bit of blackfella in him the way he carries on but he'd never admit it. You'll never see Harry on a horse though. Not since he got tossed by a little mare of his. Couldn't ride a gate on a windy day! Suits me, the mare's a beauty and I get to ride it now.

NAOMI: And what am I going to do?

ROBBIE: Work for the Mrs. You know, cook and all that stuff. Don't worry, you'll be right. I wouldn't let you go there if I didn't think you'd be right.

NAOMI: But what about this?

She pats her pregnant tummy.

ROBBIE: Mrs loves kids. 'Specially babies. Don't worry, it's all arranged. Trust me.

NAOMI: I do Robbie.

ROBBIE: Let's enjoy tonight eh? We're not that far from town, I'll put you on the train in the morning. You'll be right Sis.

The kids run in.

KARINA: Mum! We saw a whole mob of roos across the river.

BETTINA: Yeah. Hundreds of them. You gotta climb up the tree to see them though.

NAOMI: They come down to the river for a drink and a feed.

BETTINA: Dinner before bedtime, eh Mum?

NAOMI: Something like that.

ROBBIE: You kids know the kangaroo dance?

KARINA: No.

BETTINA: Can you teach us Uncle Robbie?

ROBBIE: I reckon I can. Here.

ROBBIE teaches the kids the kangaroo dance. The kids join in.

BETTINA: Come on Mum.

NAOMI tries but it is a difficult dance for a pregnant woman.

NAOMI: That's enough of that, I don't want my joey popping out early!

ROBBIE: Time for a feed eh?

KARINA: Yes please I'm starving.

BETTINA: Me too.

ROBBIE: Try some good bush tucker.

The kids try some.

BETTINA: This' good.

KARINA: Tastes like chicken.

ROBBIE: Probably ate a chicken!

NAOMI: Yum this sure beats bully beef.

KARINA: What is it Uncle Rob?

ROBBIE: What do you think it is?

KARINA: I dunno.

ROBBIE: Could be a sheep, could be a chook. Could even be an elephant. Isn't though. It's that snake that nearly ate ya.

The kids nearly faint.

ROBBIE: Best tucker you'll ever eat.

NAOMI: That's right.

ROBBIE: Look at those stars, see that there looks like a pot, if you ever get lost you just follow that.

BETTINA: Where?

NAOMI: There.

She points out the stars to the girls.

ROBBIE: Now you girls settle down there and I'll tell you a yarn. When I was a young fella and your mum was only a baby my dad taught me the most important lesson I've ever learnt. One day we were wandering along the street, just minding our own business, when we heard this racket. Well, the old man, he was always interested in what was goin' on, so we race around the corner to where the racket's coming from. Well, strike me pink if there wad this fella, a big fella with a big ugly nose, there he was fairly laying into his horse. He was giving it larry dooley. Thrashing it with his reins. Well, the old man didn't like that at all.

'What do you think you're doin'?' he says.

'None of your bloody business you black bastard,' says the ugly bloke. 'You keep out of it or I'll give you a thrashing too.'

Well, the old man didn't like that. Quick as a flash he jumped on this bloke and gave him the belting he deserved. He could go like a thrashing machine when he was stirred up, and I tell you what he was stirred up that day. He fairly flattened him.

He demonstrates.

Left hooks, right hooks, uppercuts, jabs. He destroyed the rotten mongrel. I was pretty impressed. He turned to me and he said, 'Whatever you do son, never be cruel to dumb animals. You can fight any man you want to and he can fight back but an animal can't fight back.'

So never, ever lift your hand to a dumb animal.

NAOMI: Come on kids, time for a sleep, we got a big day tomorrow. We're going to catch the train.

The kids snuggle up and go to sleep. ROBBIE *and* NAOMI *sit quietly as the sounds of the night surround them.*

God this is beautiful.

ROBBIE: Sure is Sis.

NAOMI: It's so peaceful.

ROBBIE: Yeah.

NAOMI: Wish we could stay here forever Rob. If we could bottle this moment and keep it and never have to leave.

ROBBIE: Huh.

NAOMI: Look at those kids, don't they look innocent? Sometimes, when I put them to bed I watch them, and I wonder how it is they're the same kids that get into so much trouble and get me so stirred up.

ROBBIE: They've got it made, kids.

NAOMI: Yeah, shame we have to grow up.

ROBBIE: Yeah.

NAOMI: Well, some of us. Some never bother do they Rob?

ROBBIE: Sis, I'll be a kid for as long as I can get away with it!

NAOMI: True.

ROBBIE: We better get some sleep ourselves, big day tomorrow.

NAOMI: You're a true friend bro, I'll never forget this. Tell you what though, you had me worried. Thought you were going to leave me on that Mission.

ROBBIE: I wouldn't do that would I? We're family.

NAOMI: True. We are. Family.

THAT ONCE WAS MINE

NAOMI: [*singing*]

    Law just has no meaning. Things I can't define
    As I stand upon this land. That once was mine

    Fools that had no feelings
    For what this country meant
    As I stand upon this land
    That's now covered by cement
    And I still walk upon this land
    That once was mine… that once was mine

    And the protests we made
    They refused to recognize
    They thought that they knew more
    They thought that they were civilised
    With guns they chased me from my land

Law just has no meaning. Things I can't define
As I stand upon this land. That once was mine

The past has taught us distrust
Their promises all lies
And the government has fenced off
All this land that once was mine
They say I trespass on this land
That once was mine. That once was mine

SCENE FOUR

At Bin Bin Station four years later. NAOMI *has established herself as the chief housekeeper on Bin Bin Station. She is the boss of the kitchen. She happily decorates a birthday cake.*

NAOMI: 'Happy Birthday Rose'. There you go! Now...

> *She checks the stove, stirring and then tasting a stew.*

Not bad. Ahh... candles!

> *She goes to the pantry as* ENID, *the property owner's wife enters.*

ENID: Naomi?
NAOMI: [*off*] Yes Mrs?
ENID: I... what are you doing in there?
NAOMI: [*off*] Looking for some candles.

> *She enters.*

That pantry is a disgrace! If we don't do something about it it'll be full of rats.
ENID: Lovely cake.
NAOMI: I can't find the candles.
ENID: I'll get them, I know where they are.
NAOMI: You been in there 'rearranging' again?
ENID: I was looking for some castor oil.
NAOMI: Oh?
ENID: Mr Boulder's been a bit, you know... constipated.
NAOMI: It's not my cooking is it?
ENID: No! Of course not! You know him, he gets himself so knotted up.

They both laugh. ENID *goes to find the candles. The sound of boxes being upturned can be heard.*

NAOMI: Now I *will* have to clean it up!

ENID: [*off*] Rosie's still down with the women?

NAOMI: Yeah.

More sounds of crashing boxes. NAOMI *smiles to herself.*

ENID: [*off*] Found them!

She enters triumphantly holding the candles.

There!

NAOMI: Well done!

ENID: Shouldn't she be home?

NAOMI: Not yet, give me a chance to get some work done.

ENID: I could look after her.

NAOMI: She's fine.

ENID: Don't you… well, you know, worry…

NAOMI: About what?

ENID: Oh, the, ah… the women.

NAOMI: Why?

ENID: Well, they're not all that clean are they?

NAOMI: What?

ENID: I mean… the babies… their noses are always runny!

NAOMI: Mrs Boulder, those women are Rosie's people. Our people.

ENID: Yes. Yes. Of course, but do you think it's right?

NAOMI: What?

ENID: Your children playing with the stockman's children.

NAOMI: 'Course it's right, they're having fun and they're playing with their people, what could be righter?

ENID: But won't they pick up bad habits?

NAOMI: Only from gubbas… Nah! Look, its important that they know who they are. Them women down the creek, they know a lot, important stuff, stuff they need to learn. Now make yourself useful and put the candles on the cake will you?

ENID: Oh yes, I'd be delighted.

She carefully places candles as NAOMI *returns to the stew.*

I was thinking, we better use up the rest of that mutton before it goes off. Mr Boulder's going to kill tomorrow so we'll have some fresh meat.

NAOMI: I already have.

ENID: What?

NAOMI: Used the mutton.

She indicates the stew.

ENID: The girls should be home from school shouldn't they?

NAOMI: Should be. Just think, Rosie'll be joining them there soon...

ENID: Amazing how time flies. Oh, by the way Naomi...

NAOMI: Yes Mrs Boulder?

ENID: Enid. Call me Enid.

NAOMI: Yes Mrs Boulder.

ENID: I mean it's quite ridiculous really. We've known each other all this time, you can't go on calling me Mrs Boulder.

NAOMI: Yes Mrs Boulder.

ENID *laughs. They have an easy, friendly relationship.*

I'm sorry, Mrs Enid... I mean Enid. Oh! I can't get out of the habit! Anyway, can you imagine what your husband would say if he overheard me calling you Enid, he'd have me horsewhipped.

ENID: Don't take any notice of him.

NAOMI: Easy for you...

ENID: I'm sorry, that was a silly thing to say.

NAOMI: You know how he carries on.

ENID: He's all puff and wind. His bark's worse than his bite.

NAOMI: Yeah, well... I've been bitten once too often.

There is an awkward pause which ENID *relieves by pulling out a beautiful pink dress which she has bought for the four year old* ROSE.

ENID: What do you think?

NAOMI: Oh... it's beautiful. You, you shouldn't have...

ENID: Why not? You know how much I adore her.

NAOMI: She'll love it. It'll look lovely on her.

ENID: She's such a gorgeous little thing.

NAOMI: Takes after her Mum eh?... Thank God!

NAOMI *returns to the stew.* ENID *watches her for a moment.*

ENID: What about her Dad?

NAOMI: Pass the salt will you?

She does and NAOMI *adds salt to the stew.*

ENID: You never talk about him.

NAOMI: I never talk about a lot of things.

ENID: You shouldn't be so secretive Naomi.

NAOMI: Don't you have something to do?

ENID: Oh. I'm sorry... actually, I did want your advice on something.

NAOMI *stops stirring and looks at her.*

NAOMI: You're right.

ENID: Pardon?

NAOMI: I'll have to tell her. Won't I?

ENID: What?

NAOMI: About her father. She'll want to know.

ENID: Yes, yes, I suppose she will. But you don't have to tell me. It's none of my business.

NAOMI: He was white.

Pause

It was after Les took off. He promised to look after us. To take us off the Mission. He lied to me.

ENID: Oh, Naomi, I'm sorry.

NAOMI: I never told you because I was ashamed... I didn't want to remember him. But you have to... I dunno, face it, don't you? You can't pretend it never happened. You know what? Every birthday I think about it. I wish I didn't but I do...

ENID *comforts her.*

Ahh! This' no good. I've gotta be in a good mood for Rosie on her birthday haven't I? Here! Wasn't there something you wanted to ask me?

ENID: Yes, that's right. I'm going into town and I wondered if you could help me decide which dress to wear, I can't make up my mind.

NAOMI: All right, but get a move on. Dinner won't cook itself.

ENID *rushes off*

Nothing better to do than worry about which dress to wear! Still,
she's all right, for a gubba.

*BETTINA and KARINA rush in from school. They are now nine
and twelve.*

KARINA: Hi Mummy!

NAOMI: Hello darlin', have a good day?

BETTINA: Yeah! I won the 100 metres and the long jump!

NAOMI: Well done!

BETTINA: And Mr Beecher reckons I can be in the school play as long
as I have a note saying it's okay.

NAOMI: Uh huh.

KARINA: And *I* got a gold star Mummy, for tidying up.

NAOMI: Good girl.

BETTINA: Can we go down the creek?

NAOMI: Yes, and bring Rosie back. Time for her party!

KARINA: I did a painting for her Mummy.

NAOMI: All right, off you go. And no swimming today! I want you back
here before it gets dark.

BETTINA: Let's go.

NAOMI: Bettina! You hear me? Straight back.

BETTINA: Yes Mum.

NAOMI: Go on, off you go.

They go as ENID rushes in with two dresses and holds one up.

ENID: Well?

NAOMI: That's a pretty colour.

ENID: You think so?

NAOMI: Suits you.

ENID: What about this one?

NAOMI: It's nice too.

ENID: Naomi?

NAOMI: Yes?

ENID: The tone in your voice tells me something.

NAOMI: Well, which one do you like?

ENID: This one.

She holds up the second dress. NAOMI *works on.*

NAOMI: Oh.

ENID: And?

NAOMI: Well, I tell you, you go wearing that and you'll have every fella in town staring at you.

ENID: Maybe I should…

NAOMI: Eh, you behave.

ENID: I'll wear this one then. Harry Boulder's wife can't be seen to do the wrong thing can she?

NAOMI: It suits you better anyway.

ENID: Thank you.

>*She puts the dresses away and fusses around preparing for the birthday…*

ENID: These cups will be best.

NAOMI: When you going to have one?

ENID: A what?

NAOMI: A bubby.

ENID: I don't know.

NAOMI: You ought to get a move on you know, you're not getting any younger.

ENID: Thanks Naomi. I'm not sure I can.

NAOMI: Can what?

ENID: Have a baby.

NAOMI: Why not?

ENID: Well, don't tell Mr Boulder, but I've been trying.

NAOMI: You need help you know.

ENID: I do know how babies are made.

NAOMI: Well?

ENID: Nothing's happened.

NAOMI: Hasn't old Mr Boulder got any sting in him.

ENID: It might be me.

NAOMI: I never had any trouble, every time I looked sideways at a man I seemed to get pregnant.

ENID: I wish I could have a baby.

NAOMI: I know what you need Mrs, you need a blackfella!

>ENID *laughs as* NAOMI *works on busily.*

NAOMI: When you going into town?

ENID: Later. I've got a Committee Meeting for the Picnic Races, and
after that we're having a meeting about the fete and I thought I might
drop in on Mrs Lee for a cup of tea.

NAOMI: That should keep you busy.

ENID: Anything I can do?

NAOMI: Set the table if you like, just don't get in the way.

She does. NAOMI *laughs.*

ENID: I'll try not to.

NAOMI: Just gammin'. Tell you the truth, I like the company. The more
kids grow up the less they seem to need you, or that's what they
think. Lookout! We keep yapping we'll never get this party ready!

As they work ENID *begins humming* The Lullaby. NAOMI *picks it
up and they sing it together.*

LULLABY

NAOMI: [*singing*]
Buluring goother, bimble and biram in your eyes my goother
Girl, child, land and sky in your eyes my child
Yindi is sleeping, marloo, tiddalick and berrimilla now must
rest
*Sun is sleeping, kangaroo, frog and kookaburra now must
rest*
Biara is watching, so sleep my buluring goother
Moon is watching, so sleep my girl child

NAOMI: It's a long time since we sung that.

The moment is broken by HARRY BOULDER's *entrance.*

HARRY: Oh, there you are Enid, I've been looking for you everywhere.
Now, look here, I've just got a message that Percy Buttons is coming
into the District and I want to throw a dinner party for him and his
entourage. That's his 'party'.

ENID: When?

HARRY: At the weekend. Now we'll need to get stuck in, I want this to
be a spectacular event.

ENID: Why?

HARRY: Because Enid, Percy Buttons is the Speaker of The NSW Legislative Assembly. A very influential person. Some Crown land is becoming available. We're never going to expand unless we get hold of some of those river flats.

ENID: But…

HARRY: Now I suggest you speak to the Ridges and ask if we can borrow their cook for a few days.

ENID: Why?

HARRY: Well we can't have blackie here doing it can we? I mean, the Buttons party will be expecting more than mutton stew won't they? The Ridge's cook trained in Paris.

> NAOMI *and* ENID *are stunned by this.*

Well? That's settled then. See to it won't you Enid? Blackie can have a day off or maybe we should swap her with the Ridges, although they'll be dining with us. Whatever.

> *He goes to leave.*

NAOMI: Hang on a sec.

HARRY: Yes blackie?

NAOMI: This' my kitchen.

HARRY: What?

NAOMI: This' my kitchen and no-one else is gonna cook in my kitchen.

HARRY: I beg your pardon.

NAOMI: You heard me. If another cook sets foot in this kitchen I'll be out that door before she's had a chance to unpack her bag.

HARRY: You'll do as you're told. No-one tells me what to do.

NAOMI: Well then, you can make up my pay now. I'll go and pack my things and pick up the kids. I don't play second fiddle to anyone. Not in my kitchen.

ENID: Naomi, please…

NAOMI: If you think I'm going to stand around listening to this, you've got rocks in your head.

> NAOMI *angrily leaves.*

ENID: Well, isn't that a fine mess.

HARRY: What's got into her? Have a talk to her will you and tell her something about respect while you're at it.

ENID: Wait on Harry.

HARRY: What? Come on hurry up. I've got work to do.

ENID: What's wrong with Naomi's cooking? She's cooked for us for two years and none of us has ever been sick.

HARRY: Enid, she's a very good country cook but really and truly can you imagine her cooking for people of this ilk?

ENID: You worry too much Harry, you'll give yourself another ulcer. I trust Naomi to cook our food anytime and for anyone.

HARRY: Oh really Enid, you're missing the point! I've got an enormous amount to think about…

ENID: All you've got to do is to make sure you invite all the right people and leave the rest to us.

HARRY: No Enid, it's not good enough. Just not good enough.

ENID: I tell you what Harry Boulder, if Naomi leaves I'll be right behind her.

HARRY: I beg your pardon?

ENID: She's a good friend. You're always off somewhere doing something terribly important. Who do you think I talk to?

HARRY: You've got the neighbours.

ENID: The neighbours! They're miles away and even if they were closer who'd want to spend their time discussing the latest way to crochet or how to make a perfect sponge. That Emily Ridge is as thick as a post.

> NAOMI *storms back.*

ENID: Oh, Naomi…

NAOMI: And another thing Mr Boulder, you don't seem to have any trouble eating seconds do you? My cooking not good enough!

ENID: Naomi, Mr Boulder would like you to bake a leg of pork for the dinner. That's your speciality isn't it?

NAOMI: Yes, amongst others.

ENID: He realises how great your contribution has been and in the light of our magnificent wool clip, he has decided that it is time to raise your pay.

HARRY: I…

ENID: Harry dear, you don't think I should visit Mother this weekend do you?

HARRY: No, I would like you to be here to look after Mrs Buttons and the other ladies.

ENID: Exactly. Mr Buttons will be delighted that he chose to eat with us won't he Naomi?

NAOMI: Oh yes Mrs Enid, he'll never have a better feed as long as he lives. You can tell him that for me Mr Boulder.

HARRY: Yes. Well, yes, I, I will.

ENID: We owe you an apology don't we Harry? We didn't mean to offend you. We were a bit confused because Mr Buttons is such an important person and we're a bit anxious about doing the right thing aren't we dear?

HARRY: Yes, well I'll leave it up to you then Enid. I trust you've made the right decision.

ENID: Besides, there is another event of equal significance which needs to be adressed before we can worry about Percy Buttons.

HARRY: Eh?

ENID: Our Rosie's birthday. Now, you'd better hurry along dear we don't want to keep you any longer.

HARRY: Right. Good.

ENID: Shall we say four pound a month then?

HARRY: Ahhh, yes. All right.

> HARRY *departs making as dignified as exit as possible under the circumstances.*

NAOMI: Well you certainly put a spoke in his wheel didn't you?

ENID: Talk about women fussing! What a performance, men are such peacocks aren't they?

NAOMI: Some are peacocks and some are worms and some are like the brown snake, you take your eyes off them and they strike.

ENID: We'll need to kill a pig…

NAOMI: I'll get the boys onto it straight away.

ENID: Good.

NAOMI: That Percy Buttons is in for a treat, I hope he deserves it!

SCENE FIVE

> ENID *and* NAOMI *parody the guests at the Big Dinner.*

WALTZ

NAOMI: [*singing*]
> Enid my dear, the meal was divine, and so was the wine

ENID: [*singing*]
> Sir Percy you're rotten, take your hand off my bottom

NAOMI: [*singing*]
> I'm sorry, I forgot we're refined
> Please call me Joan, Yes we own land, Free title you understand

ENID: [*singing*]
> Enough talk of farce, you've got a nice arse

NAOMI: [*singing*]
> Sir remove your hand

ENID: [*singing*]
> Harry I'm very impressed, and how charming this evening you look

NAOMI: [*singing*]
> My lady, nice view, I'd do anything for you

ENID: [*singing*]
> So why don't you find us a nook
> I loved the baked chook
> Can I meet the cook

NAOMI: [*singing*]
> You can't fool me
> She's from Paris

ENID: [*singing*]
> Attention my sweets, Here's someone to meet

NAOMI: [*singing*]
> Who deserves a pat on the back

ENID: [*singing*]
> Naomi, come here, our chef without peer

NAOMI and ENID: [*singing together*]
> Oh my God, Sir Percy, she's black!

SCENE SIX

A few days later. NAOMI *is happily working in the kitchen, mixing a cake.*

NAOMI: I hope this works out all right, Enid'll be hungry after all that travelling and no-one likes a cake as much as she does.

She casually looks out the window and then suddenly sees something.

Rose! You get out of that puddle! You'll dirty your nice clean dress. Go on! Get out of it! Go and play with your sisters. Bettina! Keep an eye on Rosie will you? Ohhh. Look at them.

She returns to her work humming the lullaby we heard in the last scene. ENID *enters.*

NAOMI: Oh, you're up! Cake's not ready yet. I thought you'd have a lie down after such a long journey. How was the city?

ENID: Pretty depressing I'm afraid.

NAOMI: All those people rushing about. Like a bunch of chooks with their heads cut off if you ask me.

ENID: Yes.

NAOMI: Are you all right?

ENID: Yes. I'm just a bit… tired.

NAOMI: That all?

ENID looks at NAOMI before she speaks.

ENID: Do you know why I went to the city? I've been having a series of tests done.

Pause.

They've confirmed what I've always suspected. I can't have a baby.

NAOMI: Oh no. [*She stops work*] That's terrible. I had no idea that's what you were talking about before… you know, when you said… Oh, Mrs, that's sad. You should get a second opinion though, they're not always right those doctors, they may think they're God but…

She goes to comfort ENID who pulls away.

ENID: You know how desperately I want a family. I've been talking to some people and they suggest I adopt a baby.

NAOMI: Well, why don't you then?

ENID: It's not quite as simple as that.

Pause

What would you say if I said I was thinking of adopting an Aboriginal baby?

NAOMI: Eh?

ENID: Well… not fully Aboriginal…

NAOMI: What are you getting at?

ENID *blurts out…*

ENID: Naomi, I want to adopt Rosie.

NAOMI: What?

ENID: I want to adopt Rosie. I've known her all her life, I've cared for her and I can give her a future.

NAOMI: Enid…

ENID: Naomi, I can give her a start in life, I can assure her of a good education and some security in the world.

NAOMI: You're talking about my baby. My Rosie…

ENID: Listen, I've thought this through very carefully. She's still young enough. You'd obviously be able to see her and it would take the pressure off you a bit. I'd make money available so that you can really give the older girls a chance. It would all be in writing. I've spoken to my stockbroker and he suggested I sign some share scrips over to you. Think about it.

NAOMI *is stunned.*

We would still be close, your family would still be together and in the long run everyone would be better off.

Pause. NAOMI *turns away, unable to comprehend what she is hearing.*

Even the Adoption Agency people agree. The Protection Board are behind me. They think it's the most humane thing to do for those who don't belong…

NAOMI: Don't belong?

ENID: Well… what I mean is… I'm only thinking of Rosie.

Pause. NAOMI *is unable to speak as* ENID *pulls papers out of her bag.*

Look, I've got the papers here for you to have a look at. You can take your time to think about it but I'm sure you'll see what a wonderful thing this will be for everyone involved.

NAOMI: You must be out of your mind.

ENID: Think about it Naomi.

NAOMI *turns on her.*

NAOMI: I don't need to think about it. You must be mad! I wouldn't part with my children for anything. Anything! I thought you were a friend.

ENID: I am Naomi, don't you see what I'm offering you? A chance for Rosie to make it in the world. I'm offering you the chance to give your daughter a future.

NAOMI: You make me sick! You get out of here. Go on. Get out of my sight. I've never been so insulted in all my life. You're worse than the Mission Manager. You're… get out, get out of here, just go…

ENID *escapes.*

And don't you go anywhere near my children ever again. You hear me!

SCENE SEVEN

Night. NAOMI *is packing her things.* ROBBIE *helps her.*

ROBBIE: Jeez Sis, I seem to spend half my life moving you.

NAOMI: Shhh.

ROBBIE: It's all right, no-one's awake. Yet. Come on. Those kids won't keep quiet in the car for long.

NAOMI: I don't want to leave anything…

ROBBIE: Come on! Everything you need is in the car.

NAOMI: I can't find Rosie's teddy.

ROBBIE: She's got it with her. This' mad, you're a free person, this isn't the Mission you know.

NAOMI: I want to be out of here and well away before they realise we've gone.

ROBBIE: Whatever you reckon Sis.

NAOMI: Here. Grab this.

She loads him up with belongings then mutters to herself.

No-one's gonna take my baby away from me.

ROBBIE: You got any money?

NAOMI: Enough.

ROBBIE: Well you can stay with me but I tell you Sis, it's not exactly

Buckingham Palace.

NAOMI: It'll do.

ROBBIE: You gonna find it tougher than you think. Them city bullymen don't like blackfellas much. You gotta be careful.

NAOMI: I'm not a child.

ROBBIE: But you don't know nothing. I'm worried about you going to the city. You'd be better off in the bush.

NAOMI: We'll manage.

ROBBIE: Just keep away from the Welfare, they've got some bad habits. If that missus Enid wants to she can make things pretty tough for you.

NAOMI: I know. That's what I'm worried about.

ROBBIE: Let's get a move on.

> HARRY *enters, accompanied by a distraught* ENID. *They have been in bed.*

HARRY: What the hell's going on here?

ROBBIE: I told you we shoulda hurried.

ENID: This isn't the answer Naomi. Surely we can work something out?

NAOMI: Come on Robbie.

HARRY: What's he got to do with it?

ROBBIE: Family, Harry, something you gubs don't know much about.

HARRY: Look here Robbie, you might know a bit about horses but…

ROBBIE: No time to talk Harry, we got a train to catch.

ENID: Naomi?

ROBBIE: Come on Sis.

HARRY: Now you listen here…

ROBBIE: No. You listen. We may not have the vote but we're still free to go where we want to.

ENID: Wait Naomi, have you got any money, where are you going to stay?

NAOMI: Goodbye Enid.

ENID: Do something!

HARRY: Ahh, wait.

> ROBBIE *blocks the doorway.*

ROBBIE: Sorry, only room for us on this trip.

ENID: For Christ's sake Harry! Do something for once in your life…

HARRY: I, ah… look be reasonable, you've got no money to speak of…

ROBBIE: Remember Harry, you pull a horse too hard and it'll throw you in the end.

He rushes off. HARRY *shouts after him.*

HARRY: You'll regret this… I promise you.

ENID *turns on* HARRY.

ENID: You useless bloody idiot! Look what you've done now!

HARRY: But… Enid. It's not my fault…

She storms off.

Damn you Naomi!

He shouts after them

You won't get away with this Naomi. You mark my words. You won't get away with this! This won't be the end of it… You hear me?

END OF ACT ONE

ACT TWO

SCENE ONE

Redfern, Sydney 1991. A Street Scene with many characters from Redfern; a celebration of life in Redfern which mirrors the beginning of Act One. The Song involves the whole Company. At the end of the song ROSE *enters. She is a young adult.*

REDFERN SONG

ALL: [*singing*]
chorus   Redfern is our place
City of koorie culture
Living in the shadows
of business vultures
200 years, we're still here
We're still here

Media shows Redfern under siege
TNT, TV, police brutality
And they say this country is free
Down and out in the city

Hear us speak in one voice
Legal aid for community
Striving for equality
will stop the use of force

Repeat *chorus*

Medical service fills a need
Gone are years we won't forget
Koories beating past neglect
Years of fighting corporate greed

Repeat *chorus*

As the Company disperse a few 'drinkers' are left behind.
They pass round a bottle of plonk. One of them is ROBBIE. *He*
is nineteen years older and has been living hard and is hardly
recognizable from the ROBBIE *of Act One.* ROSE *approaches.*

ROBBIE: How're goin'!

ROSE: Oh, I'm well thank you.

ROBBIE: Good on ya darlin', like a drop of 'Nellie Bligh'?

ROSE: No thank you.

ROBBIE: Suit yourself.

ROSE: Actually, I'm looking for Betty's Bargains.

ROBBIE: What?

ROSE: Betty's Bargains. It's a shop.

ROBBIE: Oi! Any of you mob heard of, what the fuck did you call it?

ROSE: Betty's Bargains.

ROBBIE: Betty's Bargains.

The drinkers mumble responses. Three Aboriginal girls on their
way to work approach and playfully hassle ROSE.

Hey, this girl here, she's lookin' for Betty's Bargains.

SHARON: What do you want to go there for?

ROSE: There's a big sale there. Country Road specials.

SHARON: You got a quid have you?

ROSE: Pardon.

SHARON: Well, we don't exactly shop there do we girls?

TRICIA: Not unless we win Lotto.

CATHY: The pension don't stretch that far does it?

SHARON: Nuh. Only gubs can afford to shop at Betty's Bargains.

TRICIA: Yeah, gubs from up town with a purse full of coins, eh Shaz?

CATHY: That's right Sis.

ROBBIE: You gonna tell this girl where to go or what?

SHARON: Lend me a dollar Sis.

TRICIA: Yeah, how about a dollar or two.

CATHY: Then we can go down to Country Road and get ourselves all
    dolled up like you.

SHARON: Or maybe even slip down to the pub for a drink.

TRICIA: Or score some yandi.

She indicates a 'joint'.

CATHY: Or both.

SHARON: Yeah, maybe you'd like to shout us, eh Sis?

TRICIA: Good idea Shaz.

CATHY: Tell you what, I'm dying for a feed and a drink, the pension doesn't go far you know.

SHARON: Sure doesn't.

TRICIA: We get pretty desperate. Look at all those lazy blackfellas, think they'd have something better to do with their time, all that sitting around doing nothing, never know what they might get up to.

CATHY: You gotta be careful in Redfern Sis.

ROSE: I, ah, I better be going. Thanks for your help.

The girls smile disarmingly.

SHARON: Hey don't worry darlin' we're just gammin.

TRICIA: It's over there, round the corner and past the bank.

ROSE: Thanks. You had me worried there for a sec.

SHARON: Think we were going to roll you eh?

TRICIA: Knock you off and flog your wallet eh?

CATHY: Typical blackfellas eh? Just waiting to roll a gub.

ROSE: I didn't say that.

SHARON: But you meant it.

ROSE: No I didn't.

CATHY: You be careful babe, our day's comin'.

SHARON: Yeah. You've had nearly 200 years, gonna be our turn soon.

CATHY: That's right, you watch out, we might start asking for our land back.

TRICIA: Come on girls let's go, we'll be late for work.

SHARON: See? We're on the way up!

They laugh and leave waving as they go. ROSE *is stunned.*

ROBBIE: Here Sis I'll show you. Hold on...[*peering into her face*] Bloody hell, the Nellie Bligh's playin' tricks with me brain. Come on darlin'.

A film crew moves in. BETTINA, *now thirty-one, is the star; everyone is deferential to her.*

What's goin' on here?

ROSE: Looks like a film crew.

ROBBIE: Ahh bugger them, come on I haven't got all day you know.

ROSE: I'll be right thanks, I'm sure I can find it now.

ROBBIE: Okay. You look after yourself.

> *She goes to leave.*

Hey! You ever need someone to show you round… I'll be here. This' my place.

ROSE: Yeah… thanks.

ROBBIE: Lot of you Murries get lost round here and get into strife…

ROSE: Murrays? My name's not Murray.

ROBBIE: Streuth. I gotta go on the wagon.

> *He wanders off.* ROSE *goes to leave but is captivated by the film crew. She moves to the side and watches.*

DIRECTOR: Ok, let's get this happening.

ASSISTANT Do you want to set up here?

DIRECTOR: Yep. Let's get cracking.

ASSISTANT Right guys, over here. Are the actors ready?

DIRECTOR: Of course. Tim, I want this to look real, all right? We're not making some soap opera here are we?

> *There is frenzied activity; actors being made up, camera crew lining up shots,* BETTINA *is the centre of attention.*

ASSISTANT: Okay. Are we ready? I don't want any stuff-ups here. We've only got this location for an hour. Mind your backs!

> *Crew move through with props.*

DIRECTOR: Tim, I want to go straight into this. We've run the lines and had a couple of good rehearsals. Bettina wants to go straight into it. Let's get it while they're hot.

ASSISTANT: Sure. Okay you guys. We're gonna go straight into this. Put one down straight away. Quiet! A bit of quiet please!

DIRECTOR: Thanks Tim. Right. Remember where you are. You are not in suburbia, all right. You are in a shanty town. You are not middle-class blacks, you are battlers. You don't have much money, there's no pension. You've had the shit beaten out of you so these people are a threat. They come from another place. I want to see it in your eyes. Remember where it comes from. The centre. Here. [*He thumps his chest.*]

DIRECTOR: Let's do it.

ASSISTANT: Ready? Okay, Bettina you right darling?

> BETTINA *steps forward. She is playing an old lady, many years ago.*

BETTINA: Can I have a glass of water please?

> *The* ASSISTANT *gives her one.*

ASSISTANT: Right darling?

BETTINA: Thanks.

ASSISTANT: This is it. Quiet please.

> *There is absolute silence.* ROSE *is transfixed by all this.*

Roll camera.

SOUND: Speed.

CAMERA OPERATOR: Roll 10, scene 57, take one.

DIRECTOR: And... Action!

> *In the scene* BETTINA's *baby is taken away by a* NURSE.

BETTINA: You're not takin' my baby, no-one takes my baby.

NURSE: Come on love, just do as you're told.

BETTINA: No...

NURSE: Be reasonable, we don't want any trouble love.

BETTINA: My baby.

NURSE: Are you going to hand it over or am I going to have to take it?

BETTINA: Please...

NURSE: Look here, love, it'll be easier in the long run if we get this over quickly.

BETTINA: *No!*

> *She grabs her baby and hugs her desperately. A man's voice is provided off-camera by the* DIRECTOR.

MAN'S VOICE: Come on Matron, we haven't got all day.

> *The* NURSE *tries to grab the baby. They struggle.*

BETTINA: Leave me alone.

NURSE: It's for the best dear.

MAN'S VOICE: You wanna hand Matron?

BETTINA: You can't take my baby, you can't.

NURSE: Tiny!
NURSE: [*calling off camera*] I need help! I warned you, you silly girl!
DIRECTOR: And… cut.

Everyone relaxes. An assistant attends to BETTINA.

Lovely. Very nice Bettina.
[*to the* NURSE] Vicky, I need more malevolence. Don't hold back. You're doing your job. These people are less than human to you. Patronise her. Go and get a bit more eye shadow sweetie… might help.

She goes.

All right, how was that for camera?
CAMERA OPERATOR: I think I lost focus on that last moment.
DIRECTOR: Sound?
SOUND: Fine.
DIRECTOR: Good. I'd like to go again, are you getting right in on her face for that last moment?
CAMERA OPERATOR: Yes, if Tim can keep focus.

Everyone laughs.

BETTINA: Big night last night Timmy?
ASSISTANT: Bitch!
DIRECTOR: Okay people, let's do it.
CAMERA OPERATOR: Tim. There's someone in the back there, she moved into shot on Bettina's close up.
ASSISTANT: What's going on here? Shit a brick! Excuse me sweetheart? Move out of the shot please.
ROSE: Oh. I'm sorry. I didn't… I was just watching…
ASSISTANT: Okay, but watch from over there please. Okay. Let's go again. Bettina? You right.
BETTINA: Yep. Lets do it, Vicky, don't hold back, remember rehearsal?
DIRECTOR: That's right. Let's go for it Vicky.
ASSISTANT. Will you move out of shot dearie, we're trying to shoot a film here.
ROSE: All right.

She goes to move off.

DIRECTOR: This is hopeless. We'll have to find another location.
ASSISTANT: Another one?

SCENE TWO

An office. ROSE *confronts a bureaucrat,* MISS BROWN.

ROSE: What do you mean you can't find it?

MISS BROWN: I'm sorry, there isn't any sign of it.

ROSE: Don't be stupid, there must be.

MISS BROWN: Well, there isn't.

ROSE: All I want to do is get a licence. I don't believe this.

MISS BROWN: I'm sorry, but...

ROSE: Look, I'm standing here aren't I? I'm alive. Therefore I must have been born. If I was born then there must be some record of my birth, mustn't there be?

MISS BROWN: Well, yes, theoretically.

ROSE: So where is my Birth Certificate? I can't get a licence without one.

MISS BROWN: Why don't I check your details one more time?

ROSE: Great. When I'm late back for work you can ring my boss and explain why.

MISS BROWN: Right. Name, Rose Millcroft.

ROSE: That's right.

MISS BROWN: Address, 24 Lane Street, Epping.

ROSE: Yes.

MISS BROWN: Date of Birth. 25/6/62.

ROSE: Right.

MISS BROWN: So, that makes you...

ROSE: Twenty-three.

MISS BROWN: Of course. Place of Birth?

ROSE: I told you, Epping Hospital, I think.

MISS BROWN: There isn't a maternity ward at Epping Hospital.

ROSE: I beg your pardon?

MISS BROWN: You can't have been born there.

ROSE: Well, I don't know do I?

MISS BROWN: Maybe you were born at home and your parents lost your records? Maybe...

ROSE: What?

MISS BROWN: Have you discussed this with your parents?

ROSE: No.

MISS BROWN: Do they know you're here?

ROSE: No. I'm not a child.

MISS BROWN: Of course not.

ROSE: You're the ones who lost the records. I thought this would be a simple exercise, all I want is a Birth Certificate.

MISS BROWN: I suggest you go home and ask your parents where you were born and then we can sort it out.

ROSE: I bet someone's lost the records, can't you just write one out for me, please?

MISS BROWN: That would be against the rules.

ROSE: Oh, come on, its no big deal, I'm not a criminal or anything. I want to suprise them. To do something for myself. You could write one out for me couldn't you?

MISS BROWN: Sorry, but I like my job.

ROSE: What a hassle!

SCENE THREE

ROBBIE *enters. He is very drunk and is having 'visions'.*

ROBBIE: Hey, Naomi, what you doin' here?

He peers as if seeing an apparition.

You're meant to be up bush aren't ya? Hang about, you're not Naomi. You're that girl. That's who you are.
[*to himself*] What are you bloody goin' on about! You bloody old fool.
[*Laughing*] We showed you who's Bossman, Harry Boulder. Gave you something to remember us by didn't we?
[*He drinks*] You thievin' mongrel. Go to buggery.

He drinks and laughs before he imagines he sees something.

Go away! Go on git out of here. You're dead. Finished. They told me you died. [*He drinks.*] Hey! Sis, I seen her. [*Drinking.*] What about that rotten Mission manager. We got him though didn't we boys. We sorted him right out. Me and Ronnie. Seen him in a pub near Grafton. Never forget a face, specially one that ugly!

He laughs at his joke and then is frightened.

Christ! What's that? Who's there?

He talks to the bottle.

How're ya goin' ol mate? Ahh, not too bad. No use complainin', no-one will listen to ya. Don't you ever be cruel to dumb animals. You can do what you like to Mission managers though! We did. Didn't we boys? We know all about them bastards don't we? Hold on. Who's that? You back again girl? You tryin' to haunt me? I'm gettin' outta here.

He leaves.

SCENE FOUR

Epping. ROSE *is with her parents.*

ROSE: I went into Redfern, got a beautiful top at this place called Betty's Bargains.
[*Showing the top*] Isn't it great? Love the colours! Half the price of its normal cost, must be 'cause the shop's in Redfern! Anyway, then I went back to *Birth, Deaths and Marriages* and they still had no record of my Birth Certificate. I gave this girl a hard time, she didn't know what had hit her, poor thing, but I was really angry. I gave up a game of netball to go all the way in there.

> ROSE *'s* DAD *puts down his newspaper and shows more interest than he might normally.*

MUM: Why didn't you tell us?

ROSE: What?

MUM: That you were going into Redfern.

DAD: You ought to be careful going to a place like that, you never know what might happen.

ROSE: It's all right.

DAD: There's always trouble there, you see it on the telly all the time.

MUM: Your father's right. All those riots. It's very dangerous I believe.

ROSE: Didn't seem that dangerous to me, apart from a couple of girls having a go at me, and they were only stirring.

DAD: Yeah, well you keep out of there.

ROSE: What?

DAD: You heard me.

ROSE: Come on Dad, don't be silly.

DAD: I mean it.

ROSE: I'm a big girl now, I can look after myself.

MUM: Don't get too cocky, you never know what might happen in a place like that.

ROSE: Have you ever been to Redfern?

MUM: Well, no, but I haven't been to Harlem either.

DAD: Or to Baghdad.

ROSE: Come off it.

DAD: It makes sense, why provoke trouble? There's enough trouble in life without going looking for it.

Silence. DAD *returns to his paper.*

ROSE: It's nothing like that! People there are the same as anywhere else. Just a bit friendlier if anything. There was a funny old guy who seemed to want to adopt me or something.

DAD: What?

ROSE: He offered to show me around…

DAD: Oh, adopt you as a friend…

ROSE: Yes Dad, some people are friendly you know.

MUM: You shouldn't talk to strangers…

ROSE: I actually quite liked Redfern. It was fun and energetic and I don't know, it wasn't up itself…

MUM: Rose!

ROSE: Anyway I wanted to suprise you by getting my licence but I can't because I can't find my Birth Certificate.

DAD: Oh. Look, why don't you leave it to me and I'll see what I can do.

ROSE: How?

DAD: Charlie Strachan might be able to help out.

ROSE: I don't want Charlie Strachan to help out. I'm quite capable of looking after myself. Just tell me where I was born and I'll do the rest.

MUM: You were born when we went on holidays, I've told you before.

ROSE: Yes, Mum but where? Which hospital? God, I don't know why you're making such a big deal out of it. Anyone would think I was adopted.

There is a hesitation as MUM *and* DAD *try to invent a story.*

DAD: Up the coast.

MUM: On holidays.

DAD: Your Mum was, well, she was caught short, actually.

ROSE: Caught short?

DAD: Yes, you tell her darling.

MUM: Right. Yes. Well. We were staying at, ah, Port Macquarie.

DAD: In a caravan park.

MUM: A caravan park?

DAD: Yes. You remember.

MUM: Of course I remember.

ROSE: You don't need to be so embarrassed about it.

MUM: Well, it's why we never really told you exactly.

DAD: It is a bit embarrassing really.

MUM: Yes. I was in the toilet block.

DAD: Yes.

MUM: And, well, it was late at night and I, ah, well, I got caught short.

DAD: There was a terrible panic.

MUM: Well, my waters broke, um when I was actually, um, going to the toilet.

ROSE: Jesus.

MUM: And a lady came in and I yelled out to her to get your father.

DAD: Yes, that's right.

MUM: And, well, you were born then and there.

ROSE: Jesus! Born in a toilet! Do you really expect me to believe that?

Her parents are unable to answer, they nod.

That's what I'll tell them at *Births and Deaths*? I was born in a toilet?

An embarrassed silence.

You've got to be kidding!

BELIEVING IN LIES

ROSE: [*singing*]
>Years go by the lies get worse
>But I never question why
>Maybe it's harder to face the truth
>Than to believe in lies.

Hating myself for living it
I'm too weak to change
If I entered the unknown and you turned from me
Then where would I be?

And the day that they came
I relive in my dreams
My mother knocked to the ground
And I remember her scream.

And if I wasn't such a coward
I'd try to find out why
But when you're afraid of the truth
You learn to believe in lies.

But I'll never like myself unless I try
To start living with the truth
and facing up to lies.

SCENE FIVE

Redfern. ROBBIE *is sitting alone. He takes the lid off a bottle of plonk He goes to take a swig, looks at it and then pours out the contents.*

ROBBIE: Well old mate. That's it for you, once a bloke starts seein' things it's time to straighten up a bit. Strike me pink! Now I know what the doc meant. 'I'll see you in a month,' he said, 'but you won't see me'. Didn't know what he meant. But I do now, bloody oath I do. You've been a good mate and by jeez we sure have had some fun. All those fights. Must've had a couple of hundred consecutive defeats, all of 'em with you in me corner. See you later...

He tosses his bottle away.

Good riddance to bad rubbish.

He pulls out his didgeridoo from an old hessian bag.

Now, I reckon you might be a better mate.

He plays the didgeridoo, at first a little rustily and then expertly. ROSE *enters unseen by* ROBBIE; *she stops and listens for a moment, takes out a compact and puts on some lipstick. She is caught by the sound of the didgeridoo. The Aboriginal girls enter; they are off to the footy.*

SHARON: Eh girl, you back here again?

TRICIA: Must've fallen in love with the place eh Shaz?

CATHY: Rubs off you know.

ROSE: Eh?

CATHY: Make-up.

TRICIA: Don't fool us babe.

CATHY: Can't hide forever.

SHARON: Steady on there, don't give her a hard time… who you goin' for?

ROSE: [ROSE *is confused by all this.*] Pardon?

CATHY: God this piece's thick!

SHARON: Who do you follow? You know, the footy…

TRICIA: Not the Rabbits, you're not…

CATHY: Nah, she'd go for Manly.

ROSE: Oh, I see, I forgot there was a game on today.

SHARON: Hey Unc, you comin'?

ROBBIE *stops playing and turns. He stares at* ROSE.

ROBBIE: That time already? Streuth… that bloody grog!

CATHY: Eh? Settle down Unc.

ROBBIE: That girl…

He points at ROSE.

TRICIA: Settle!

SHARON: She's all right.

CATHY: Come on, we better get a move on.

SHARON: Comin'?

ROSE: Me?

SHARON: Nah, I'm talkin' to your shadow, you wanna come with us?

ROSE: Oh, look, thanks a lot but, well, I'm a Balmain supporter myself.

CATHY: Can't help bad luck.

SHARON: Good on yer sistergirl…

ROSE: Sistergirl?

SHARON: Yeah. Listen, you looked in a mirror lately?

ROSE: What?

TRICIA: Told you she was uptown. Come on, I don't want to miss the kickoff.

CATHY: Comin' Unc?

ROBBIE: [*looking at* ROSE] Nah. I'll give it a miss today.

The girls leave happily.

You know, don't you?

ROSE: Know what? What are you talking about? What was all that 'sistergirl' stuff? What's that?

ROBBIE: I'm glad you came back.

ROSE: Why?

ROBBIE: Family.

ROSE: Oh no, look, I'm on my way to find out where I was born...

ROBBIE: You come to the right place.

ROSE: No. *Births and Deaths...* I need a licence.

ROBBIE: I'll help you.

ROSE: It's cool, I know where it is, around the corner.

She points.

ROBBIE: They're no good to you. You need family.

ROSE: What?

ROBBIE: You come back to your family...

ROSE: Oh, look...

ROBBIE *stares at her face. She turns to leave.*

ROBBIE: Don't you know?

ROSE: Know what?

ROBBIE: Who you are...

Pause.

Come here and sit down, we gotta yarn.

ROSE *tries to leave but can't. He beckons her to sit.*

Don't be afraid. I won't hurt you.

ROSE: [*sitting*] What's going on here?

ROBBIE: I know you. I know you and I know your mother.

ROSE: How?

ROBBIE: You're a black gin.

ROSE: What?

ROBBIE: You're my sister's girl.

ROSE: Don't be silly.

ROBBIE: You are girl.

ROSE: Oh, don't be ridiculous.

ROBBIE: I never forget a face, 'specially when it's family.

> *She goes to leave.*

ROSE: I've never heard anything so absurd in all my life.

ROBBIE: You were fostered out, girl.

ROSE: I'm going, I've never heard anything so stupid.

ROBBIE: Stay. Stay here and listen.

ROSE: Why, why should I listen to you? I don't even know you.

ROBBIE: You do.

ROSE: I knew I was crazy coming here again.

ROBBIE: You remember Bin Bin Station?

> *She shrugs.*

Do you?

> *She stares blankly.*

Naomi.

ROSE: Naomi?

ROBBIE: Your mother.

ROSE: My mother lives in Epping with my father.

ROBBIE: You were fostered out, girl. You were taken away from your mother when you were a little baby.

ROSE: Why should I listen to this? Why are you saying this to me? Are you trying to hurt me? I don't even know you. Why should I believe you? Look, I know you probably don't mean any harm but you have made a big mistake here. You think I'm related to you? Look at you. You're black. Aboriginal. I'm not. I'm not Aboriginal. I'm sorry but I really have to go. I wish I hadn't come here.

> *She goes to leave.*

ROBBIE: Wait, I want you to meet someone. Go and see this woman. Here's the address. She'll tell you if you don't believe me. She'll tell you about the Mission and Harry Boulder. How he reported your mother to the Protection Board. She'll tell you about the train trip, how we had to hide you under blankets and keep you quiet.

She'll tell you about the day they came and took you away. We were camped outside Brisbane. You were a tiny little thing and they just walked in and told your mother you were being neglected and they took you away. Your mother nearly died. They took you away Sis, just 'cause you were living with a mob outside the city. Just 'cause you weren't living in a 'proper house'. Someone dobbed your mother in, someone who thought they were doing the right thing by you. Someone who thought they knew best. And that someone was Harry Boulder and may he rot in hell.

ROSE: Who?

ROBBIE: Harry Boulder, the slimy mongrel dog!

ROSE: Oh look, please! I was born and raised in Epping. My parents are Keith and Jill Millcroft. This'…

ROBBIE: This' hard for you Sis and it's gonna get harder but, thank God you're comin' back. Here. Take this address. She'll help you. Trust me.

> ROSE *takes the address and reads it.*

SECRETS

ROSE: [*singing*]

> Secrets behind closed doors
> Through the angry years
> Fighting off our fears… Alone
>
> Lost in clouds of lies
> Letting no one near
> Wiping off the tears… We cry
>
> Ice cold winds of change
> They took a mother said
> Her children from their bed… Why
>
> Secrets behind closed doors
> Through the angry years
> Fighting off our fears… Alone

SCENE SIX

ROSE *approaches a house. She hesitates and then knocks. She is about to withdraw when the door opens.* BETTINA *from the filming stands, wiping her face with a towel.*

BETTINA: Yes?

ROSE: I, I uh was given this address.

BETTINA: Pardon?

ROSE: A man, he gave me this address.

BETTINA: Oh yes.

ROSE: And, uh. Well, maybe I shouldn't...

BETTINA: Excuse me, I've been doing some work on a scene, I'm not quite with it, buggered actually.

ROSE: I saw you filming in the street. The other day.

BETTINA: Oh.

ROSE: You were very good.

BETTINA: Thank you. Look, do you want an autograph or something? I don't mean to be rude but I've got an audition today and I really have a lot to do.

ROSE: I'm sorry.

BETTINA: That's all right. Normally I wouldn't worry but it's a biggie.

ROSE: I see.

BETTINA: Hang on a tic, I've got some photos lying around I could...

ROSE: I don't want an autograph.

BETTINA: Fair enough. Well, as I said, the bard awaits.

ROSE: Shakespeare?

BETTINA: Desdemona... Othello? Interesting twist don't you think? Don't know how Shakespeare would have liked it but... we Koories got to take every chance we can get, not many roles written for Koorie women you know, unless you want to be raped and beaten up all the time!

ROSE: I see.

BETTINA: Anyway been nice chatting with you... what was your name?

ROSE: Rose.

BETTINA: Rose. What a pretty... Rose. I had a...

ROSE: And you're... Bettina?

BETTINA: Yes.

ROSE: Look, I'm sorry to have taken up your time, I better be going.

BETTINA: Where you from?

ROSE: Epping.

BETTINA: Which mob?

ROSE: Eh?

BETTINA: Where you from, your mob, family, tribe?

ROSE: Oh. No. I'm, I'm not... I just came to see you, because I uh, I admire your work.

BETTINA: How old are you Rose? If you don't mind me asking.

ROSE: Twenty-two or twenty-three. It's really stupid but they seem to have lost my birth certificate, I went in to get my licence and, I mean I'm sure I'm really twenty-three.

BETTINA: You don't know where you were born?

ROSE: Not exactly, I thought it was Epping Hospital but...

BETTINA: What can you remember?

ROSE: Not a lot. Not much till I was about five or so.

BETTINA: You don't remember anything?

ROSE: No, not really...

BETTINA: And Naomi.

ROSE: That's what the guy said.

BETTINA: Which guy.

ROSE: The guy who gave me your address.

BETTINA: Robbie.

ROSE: He said I was related to him, look all this is really strange. I feel really weird, I better go. I'm sorry for taking up your time. I had no right. I...

BETTINA: Look at you.

ROSE: I better go.

BETTINA: No, wait... Oh no, this is amazing, you are, you must be. Come here.

She draws ROSE *to her and they hug.*

You'll be right bub, you'll be right. You're coming back home now. We going to sort a few things out for you. You got a lot to learn Sis. A hell of a lot to learn and a lot of it is going to hurt you real bad. But don't you worry, you're with people who'll look after you now. You're going to be all right.

ROSE: But what does this mean?

BETTINA: It means you're about to begin a journey into your soul. Don't be afraid, be grateful. This land's full of people who never learn about their Aboriginal heritage. Some are never told, some find out and don't want to know. Look at this as a gift. Oh, my baby sister, look at you…

They hug. KARINA *is heard from inside the house.*

KARINA: [*off*] Bettina, you seen my red skirt? Oh, sorry…

BETTINA: Come here 'Neen.

KAIUNA: [*off*] What?

BETTINA: Come here, quick.

KARINA *enters.*

You recognize this one?

KARINA: No.

BETTINA: Her name's Rose.

KARINA: Rose?

BETTINA: Rose. Our Rose.

KARINA: What?

BETTINA: Robbie found her.

KARINA: Really? You're our little sister?

ROSE: I don't know. I don't know what's going on. This is very…

KARINA: Confronting?

ROSE: Yes.

BETTINA: It's her.

ROSE: Look, slow down here. Even if all this is true, I'm not sure I'm ready to… I don't know what I feel.

KARINA: I knew we'd find you sooner or later, I knew it. Aren't you pretty?

She takes ROSE's *hand.*

I've thought about you every night. Every night I've prayed that you're safe and well. I've wondered what you looked like and, boy, this is pretty weird.

ROSE: Sure is.

KARINA: We've got to take you to see Mum. We'll get Robbie and head up bush. This is fantastic!

She goes to hug ROSE *who resists.*

ROSE: Hold on. I'm not at all sure about this. Please. I can't just assume a new identity.

KARINA: You'll be right Sis. Tina, we should go up tomorrow. I'll ring work, are you working?

BETTINA: I've got an audition today, that's all.

KARINA: Great. I'll see Unc and we'll hit the road. Won't Mum be excited?

ROSE: Excuse me. This isn't quite so simple. I've got a whole life, I can't just abandon…

KARINA: Don't worry about it.

ROSE: Don't worry about it!

BETTINA: She didn't mean… it's just very exciting. We've dreamed about this day and…

ROSE: Wait! I'm not sure about this at all. Okay, say I am your sister. What am I meant to do? Do you expect me to ring my parents and tell them I don't want to see them anymore? I can't do this. This isn't right, it's all too sudden. I love my parents, why should I be going behind their backs like this? They've cared for me, protected me, given me an education. Why should I doubt them?

KARINA: Please. We know what it's like. Lots of our friends…

ROSE: No you don't! You havn't got any idea. I can't suddenly become an Aboriginal. I don't know anything about it. How do you know I want to be? It's all right for you to stand there and tell me what I am and what I should be. I don't know!

She goes to leave. BETTINA *grabs her.*

BETTINA: Wait. We're going to see Mum anyway. You should come but I know how hard it is, how confusing all this is.

KARINA: We'll help you Sis.

BETTINA: [*scribbling out a note*] This is where Mum lives. We're going first thing in the morning. Come with us.

KARINA: If you can't, you know where she is so…

ROSE: I'm sorry but I can't deal with all this.

BETTINA: Here.

She gives her the note.

ROSE: I've got to go. Really.

She leaves.

SCENE SEVEN

Epping. ROSE *confronts her parents.*

ROSE: Why? You lied, you lied to me.

MUM: We didn't lie…

ROSE: Didn't lie? What was that nonsense about the caravan park?

MUM: Rose. We love you. We've raised you as our own. You must understand, we've never thought of you as anything else.

DAD: The truth is, we were frightened of losing you.

MUM: We didn't know how to tell you.

ROSE: Couldn't you trust me? Don't you know me? What an insult! What did you think I was going to do, turn my back on you? I love you. Do you understand, love you! But… you, you shouldn't have let me live a lie.

DAD: We meant to tell you Rose, we did. We were always going to, but the older you got, the harder it became…

MUM: Darling, we always wanted children, I couldn't have one…

ROSE: That's not the point, you should've told me! I could've understood that but…

Pause.

Oh, my God! How many people are out there like me, not sure of who they are or where they come from? You know what you've done to me? You've denied me… you've stopped me from knowing who I really am. Can you imagine how that feels? God. Suddenly I'm Aboriginal. Suddenly I've got… a family. Another family. Sisters I don't even know. A mother I know nothing about. What am I meant to do now? How do I become Aboriginal? Tell me! How do I do that?

Silence.

I don't belong anywhere. I'm caught in the middle.

DAD: Rose, you belong here, you always will…

MUM: This is your home. No matter what happens, no matter how…

misguided... we've been, this will always be your home.

ROSE: But you're not my real parents.

MUM *breaks down.*

The thing is, my mother, she's Aboriginal isn't she?

Pause.

Isn't she?

DAD: Yes Rose, she is.

ROSE: And that's why you didn't tell me?

DAD: No it... it isn't. It isn't the only reason.

ROSE: Oh... God!

DAD: Please, try and see it from our point of view. Please! We, didn't... think... it was... important.

ROSE: What? Are you kidding?

DAD: I don't mean...

ROSE: I'm, I'm... Aboriginal and you didn't think it was important!

DAD: Not that. I mean we always thought of you as ours, as your mother said... so we... we stupidly tried to put it out of our minds.

MUM: Darling... we do love you. Please understand that... we love you!

ROSE: I, I don't know what to do.

She takes out the piece of paper BETTINA *gave her.*

I don't know...

SCENE EIGHT

The bush. NAOMI *is chasing chooks out of the yard with her broom.*

NAOMI: Git out of here. Go on! Git out of it. Git back into your yard, messin' up my garden, what do you think it is Christmas or something? Shoo shoo. I'll sool the dogs onto you, you git into your nest and lay a few decent eggs for a change.

Exhausted by all this activity, she leans on her broom. Suddenly she shouts.

You kids! Be careful. Watch out! Bettina, look after your sister. That river's dangerous you know. Rosie! Bloody kids...

She peers into the horizon and shakes her head.

Funny getting older. Your life flashes by. Your mind goes back and forth, things jump out at you, suprise you. Some things get jumbled and become like a big melting pot. Other things come back as plain as day. I try to only really remember the good things. I'm too old to dwell on all the pain. I've had the pain and I've had the good times and... who am I kidding? You never forget. You live with the memories... you can't shake your past. Bugger it, I reckon it's time for me to move on. It's time for someone else to pick up where I left off. I don't want to hang on any longer than I have to. Everything wears out sooner or later. You chooks are lucky, you'll be eaten before you get old! You'll never have all this time to fill in. All this thinking to do. Karina! Get Rosie out of that puddle. Oh, how I miss my beautiful babies. Dear Rosie! And Bettina and Karina I hope they get something out of life. For all our troubles, sometimes I think we had more than they do. We laughed and cried and suffered and celebrated but we had our dignity. We had our rules and our beliefs. These days, I don't know what young people believe in. I just don't know. But I pray they find something and that whatever it is, it has some value. As for me, well, I reckon I've just about run my race and I'm pretty tired. Time for my nap and some lovely dreams.

She lies down on the ground covering herself with an old blanket. Humming the lullaby, she huddles up behind a tree. After a few moments ROBBIE *enters.*

ROBBIE: I dunno where she is...

BETTINA *and* KARINA *enter.*

She's usually out here.

BETTINA: No-one's inside.

ROBBIE: Look.

He finds NAOMI *sound asleep.*

Oh no... don't tell me. Sis!

There is no response.

KARINA: Mum?

ROBBIE: Sis!

BETTINA: She's not… Mum!

Still there is no response.

ROBBIE: Wake up! Please.

They stare at her briefly, then NAOMI *throws off the blanket.*

NAOMI: What's all the racket about? Can't someone even lie down and die in peace around here? What are youse staring at? Got ya! Didn't I? You thought I'd carked it! No such luck. God Bettina, what have you done to your hair? It looks terrible.

BETTINA: Thanks Mum.

NAOMI: And you Karina, you shouldn't dress like that it doesn't suit you.

KARINA: I know Mum, you've told me before.

NAOMI: Look at you Robbie, you're not nineteen any more, time you started looking after yourself.

ROBBIE: Time you stop playing games, you nearly gave me a heart attack.

NAOMI: What are you doing here anyway?

BETTINA: We've got some good news for you.

NAOMI: You've got a good part? What in?

BETTINA: No.

KARINA: It's about Rose.

NAOMI: Our Rose.

ROBBIE: Yeah Sis, we found her.

NAOMI: You found my baby, where is she?

KARINA: In the city.

BETTINA: We wanted her to come…

KARINA: But she didn't show up.

BETTINA: She's only just found out who she is.

KARINA: She was pretty freaked out Mum.

ROBBIE: So we decided to come anyway and give you the good news.

NAOMI: I want to see her, where is she?

BETTINA: Mum, a lot of people who've been adopted out, a lot of them find it really hard…

ROSE *enters.*

Oh, Mum.

NAOMI: Take me to her.

KARINA: Mum.

NAOMI: Come on. I'm going to pack.

> *She sees* ROSE.

Come on! What are you staring at?

ROSE: Mum?

NAOMI: Mum?

KARINA: You came!

ROBBIE: Good on ya Sis.

NAOMI: It's not…

BETTINA: It is.

NAOMI: Come here girl, let me look at you.

> ROSE *moves towards her, assisted by her sisters.*

Are you?

ROSE: Yes.

NAOMI: My baby…

ROSE: Yes… Mum.

NAOMI: My baby's come home.

ROSE: That's right.

NAOMI: My Rosie?

ROSE: Yes it's me. Your baby Rose.

NAOMI: Oh my God! No! Not Rosie, my baby Rosie. Bettina, get here! Is this my little Rosie? The baby they took away from me. No, I can't believe it.

ROSE: Mum.

NAOMI: Are you… oh, look at you, aren't you pretty, are you really my baby? My little baby.

ROBBIE: That's who it is Sis.

NAOMI: Oh! My baby's come home to me.

> *They hug.* NAOMI *searches* ROSE's *face re-discovering the lost child.*

ROSE: Yes, she has.

NAOMI: And I thought I'd lost you forever, I thought I'd never see you again.

ROSE: I'm home Mum.

NAOMI: Come here all of you. I, I don't know what to say.

ROBBIE: That's a first Sis.

NAOMI: Get out of it! Oh, thank you God, you haven't forgotten me after all. My family!

They hug.

WE CONTINUE TO GROW

ALL: [*singing*]
Life was my grandmother walking in the bush
'Til one day some man came changed the path that she took

chorus Land still grows sky still rains
Despite the destruction native life still remains
Sun still shines wind still blows
We've broken the chains, we continue to grow
Grow, grow, grow, Oh! Oh!

Took up their guns, laid down their laws
Justified it with their Protection Board

Repeat *chorus*

Still, everyday our children find their way home
A government law that cut too close to the bone.

Repeat *chorus*

THE END

Some Background Reading

EDWARDS, CORAL and READ, PETER (eds); *The Lost Children*, Doubleday, Moorebank NSW, 1989.

Thirteen Australians taken from their Aboriginal families tell of the struggle to find their natural parents. This book addresses the reasons behind the government action; to *re*-socialise the black children as whites and effectively create an all-white society. It examines the organisation 'Link-Up' which attempts to unite the separated families.

READ, PETER; *The Stolen Generations: The removal of Aboriginal Children in NSW 1883 to 1969*, NSW Ministry of Aboriginal Affairs - Occasional paper (No.1). Paper prepared for the Aboriginal Children's Research Project (NSW Family and Children's services Agency), 1981.

This publication outlines the various acts and policies which have greatly affected the treatment of Aboriginal families, specifically the fostering of Aboriginal children from 1883 to 1969. It provides a detailed analysis of the first official legislation; The Aborigines Protection Act of 1909, where children could be removed without parental consent in a situation where the children were found to be 'neglected', through to 1969 when The Aborigines Welfare Board was abolished.

Also addressed: employment of Aboriginals; long term effects of fostering and the attempts made by those affected to 'go home'.

REPORT OF THE WORKING PARTY OF THE STANDING COMMITTEE OF SOCIAL WELFARE ADMINISTRATORS; *Aboriginal Fostering and Adoption - Review of state and territory principals, policies and practices*, presented to the 1983 spring conference of social welfare administrators, October 1983.

An account of the more recent situation regarding the fostering and adoption of Aboriginal children. Taking into account the changing attitudes toward and heightened awareness of Aboriginal culture as being important to uphold in Aboriginal children. The assumption of the past; that it was in the child's best interest to be removed from its

Aboriginal family has been refuted. This paper reports the subsequent attempts to redress past practices through developing principles and policies. These priciples and policies emphasise the importance of retaining and supporting an Aboriginal child in their extended family and/or community and consulting with the child's family before any decision to place the child has been made.

www.ingramcontent.com/pod-product-compliance
Lightning Source LLC
Chambersburg PA
CBHW041932090426
42744CB00017B/2030